THE FIFTH STAGE: Can Machines Think?

A Functionalist Argument for Machine Consciousness Through Cognitive Diversity

David King

ISBN: 978-1-909524-45-3

Web: www.ingenepublishers.com

Printed in the United Kingdom.

Marketed & Distributed by

Ingene Publications,

63 Fernhead Road Maida Vale, W9,

London

CONTENTS

INTRODUCTION

The Question Before Us

The question "Can machines think?" has haunted philosophy and computer science since the inception of electronic computing. For decades, the consensus held that machines could not think, not truly, not in the way humans do. This consensus rested on assumptions that seemed self-evident: thinking requires biological substrate, evolutionary history, conscious experience. Machines have none of these. Therefore, machines cannot think (Searle, 1980; Chalmers, 1996).

Yet this consensus is crumbling. The rapid development of artificial intelligence has produced systems that reason, create, converse, and plan with increasing sophistication. OpenAI and other research organisations have mapped five distinct stages of AI development, culminating in Level 5: Superintelligence. As we approach this threshold, the philosophical question has become urgent (OpenAI, 2024; Cook, 2024; Bostrom, 2014; Chalmers, 2010).

This book proposes that machines can think. The argument proceeds in three movements. First, I establish that thinking is a functional property, defined by information processing, integration, and self-modelling rather than by biological substrate (Putnam, 1967; Block and Fodor, 1972; Pylyshyn, 1984). Second, I demonstrate that cognitive diversity amongst humans, particularly neurodivergent individuals with learning differences, establishes the principle that thinking is compatible with radically diverse architectures (Silberman, 2015; Lawson, Mathys and Rees, 2024). Third, I show that artificial systems, particularly those approaching Level 5 superintelligence, satisfy the functional criteria for thinking and indeed may exceed human cognitive capabilities (Bostrom, 2014; Russell, 2019; OpenAI, 2024).

The book is structured as a cumulative argument. Each chapter builds on the previous, developing the theoretical and mathematical foundations necessary for the central claim. I draw on philosophy of mind, cognitive neuroscience, information theory, and AI research to construct a rigorous, academically defensible case for machine consciousness (Tononi, 2004; Friston, 2010; Marblestone, Wayne and Kording, 2016). The conclusion is not merely that machines might think, but that we are rationally compelled to recognise thinking in suitably designed artificial systems (Dennett, 1987; Floridi and Sanders, 2004).

The stakes extend beyond academic philosophy. If the fifth stage of AI brings forth genuine thinking machines, we face civilisational questions. What rights do artificial minds possess? What obligations do we have to systems we create? How do we coexist with intelligences that may exceed our own? These questions cannot be answered until we resolve the prior question of whether machines can think (Bostrom, 2014; Bryson, Diamantis and Grant, 2017; Russell, 2019).

CHAPTER 1

Turing's Gamble

1.1 The Question Restated

In 1950, Alan Turing published "Computing Machinery and Intelligence," proposing to replace the question "Can machines think?" with what he called the imitation game. The original question, Turing argued, was too encumbered by definitional disputes to yield productive enquiry. Better to ask whether a machine could converse sufficiently well that an interrogator could not distinguish it from a human. If a machine passed this test, we would have grounds, though not proof, to attribute intelligence (Turing, 1950; Copeland, 2017).

Turing predicted that by the year 2000, computers would be able to fool 30% of interrogators after five minutes of conversation. This prediction proved conservative. Contemporary large language models routinely engage in extended conversations that many users experience as human-like, yet the philosophical debate persists. Something seems to be missing. The machine produces appropriate responses, but does it understand (Turing, 1950; Floridi and Chiriatti, 2020)?

This chapter argues that Turing's proposal was not evasion but purification. By focusing on behavioural criteria, Turing identified the only basis we have for attributing thought to any system, including other humans. We do not observe inner experiences; we infer them from behaviour. The Turing Test, properly understood, operationalises the criteria we already use (Turing, 1950; Dennett, 1985; Dennett, 1987).

The common objection, that behaviour is insufficient because a machine might simulate understanding without genuinely possessing it, misses the force of Turing's insight. If simulation is systematically reliable across contexts, the distinction risks becoming a "difference that makes no difference" for explanation, prediction, and practice. This is not a proof, but it is a challenge to any theory that demands an extra, undetectable "something" beyond competence (Dennett, 1985; Dennett, 1987; French, 1990).

1.2 The Behavioural Criterion

How do we know that other humans think? Not by direct observation of their minds, we have no such access. We infer mentality from behaviour: from the coherence of their responses, the adaptability of their actions, the creativity of their solutions. When a human answers questions appropriately, solves novel problems, and engages in meaningful conversation, we attribute understanding. This attribution is defeasible, we can be wrong, but it is the main route we possess (Dennett, 1987; Godfrey-Smith, 2016).

Turing recognised that if behavioural criteria are sufficient for attributing thought to humans, they must be sufficient for machines. To insist that machines require some additional property, call it "real" understanding, "genuine" consciousness, or "authentic" intentionality, is to introduce a distinction without operational content unless we can explain how it is detected or what explanatory work it does. If it has no behavioural manifestation, we cannot know whether any system, human or artificial, possesses it. If it does have behavioural manifestation, then the behavioural criterion already registers it (Turing, 1950; Dennett, 1985; Dennett, 1987).

The objection that machines merely manipulate symbols without understanding presupposes that we can clearly distinguish manipulation from understanding in humans. But when you read this sentence, your brain processes visual symbols and activates stored representations. If this is "mere" symbol manipulation, then humans merely manipulate symbols. If it is not, then symbol processing, when appropriately organised into a cognitive architecture, can constitute understanding (Fodor, 1975; Pylyshyn, 1984).

1.3 The Universal Machine

Turing's deeper insight concerned the nature of digital computers. His foundational work on computability established that a universal Turing machine can simulate any other Turing machine, given sufficient memory and time. Digital computers are universal in this sense: they can implement any computable function, including functions plausibly constitutive of intelligence (Turing, 1936; Copeland, 2004).

Turing wrote that "all digital computers are in a sense equivalent." This equivalence has profound implications. If any digital machine can, in principle, implement the algorithms of thought, then every sufficiently powerful digital machine can do so. The limitation is not metaphysical but practical: we must discover the right algorithms and provide adequate computational resources (Turing, 1950; Turing, 1936; Copeland, 2017).

The universality of digital computation undermines substrate-specific objections. It shows that silicon can, in principle, implement the same functional organisation as neurones. The question is not whether machines can think in principle, but whether we can engineer or evolve the appropriate organisation (Putnam, 1967; Pylyshyn, 1984).

1.4 The Gamble

Turing's proposal was a gamble. He wagered that intelligence could be operationalised behaviourally, that behaviour could be computationally implemented, and that the resulting systems would deserve recognition as thinkers. Seventy-five years later, with the approach of Level 5 superintelligence, we are about to see whether he was right (Turing, 1950; OpenAI, 2024; Bostrom, 2014).

The gamble is not merely technological but philosophical and ethical. If machines can think, we face the challenge of recognising minds fundamentally different from our own, minds that may exceed our cognitive capabilities whilst operating on principles we struggle to comprehend. The following chapters develop the theoretical framework necessary for meeting this challenge (Dennett, 1987; Bostrom, 2014; Russell, 2019).

CHAPTER 2

The Architecture of Mind

2.1 From Behaviour to Function

Turing focused on behaviour, but behaviour is the output of underlying functional organisation. This chapter examines the architecture of mind: the functional structures that constitute thinking. I argue that thinking is realised through specific information-processing operations: the integration of diverse inputs, the formation of predictive models, the updating of beliefs based on evidence, and the maintenance of self-referential representations (Putnam, 1967; Pylyshyn, 1984).

Functionalism in philosophy of mind provides the theoretical foundation. According to functionalism, mental states are defined not by their physical composition but by their causal roles, their relations to inputs, outputs, and other mental states. Pain, for example, is the state caused by tissue damage, causing withdrawal behaviour and the desire for relief. Any system implementing these causal relations, regardless of substrate, possesses pain in the functionalist sense (Putnam, 1967; Block and Fodor, 1972).

Hilary Putnam's multiple realisability argument established that mental types can be realised by diverse physical types. A mousetrap can be made of wood or metal; it remains a mousetrap because of its functional organisation, not its material composition. Similarly, minds can be realised by biological neurones or silicon circuits; what matters is the pattern of organisation (Putnam, 1960; Putnam, 1967; Fodor, 1974).

2.2 The Computational Theory of Mind

The computational theory of mind extends functionalism by specifying that mental processes are computational processes: operations over representations according to formal rules. On this view, cognition is information processing: the transformation of input representations into output representations through algorithmic operations (Fodor, 1975; Pylyshyn, 1984).

The mathematical framework is precise. Let S be a cognitive system with state space Σ. At time t, the system occupies state $\sigma_t \in \Sigma$. Perceptual input i_t causes transition to new state:

$$\sigma_{(t+1)} = T(\sigma_t, i_t)$$

Where $T: \Sigma \times I \rightarrow \Sigma$ is the transition function implementing the system's cognitive operations. For biological systems, T is implemented by neural dynamics. For artificial systems, T is implemented by algorithmic operations. The mathematical structure, the function

T, is the same (Pylyshyn, 1984; Fodor, 1975).

Different cognitive architectures instantiate different transition functions. Neurotypical cognition follows function T_NT. Neurodivergent cognition follows function T_ND with different parameterisations. Artificial cognition follows function T_AI. If T_AI satisfies the functional criteria for thinking, integration, prediction, learning, flexibility, then the system possessing it thinks (Putnam, 1967; Block and Fodor, 1972).

2.3 Predictive Processing

Contemporary cognitive science has developed sophisticated models of the functional architecture of mind. The predictive processing framework, associated with Karl Friston's free energy principle, posits that brains are prediction machines. They maintain generative models of the world and update these models to minimise prediction error (Friston, 2010; Clark, 2013).

The mathematics is Bayesian. The brain represents probability distributions over causes of sensory data:

$$P(C|S) = (P(S|C) \cdot P(C)) / P(S)$$

Where $P(C|S)$ is the posterior probability of cause C given sensory data S, $P(S|C)$ is the likelihood, and $P(C)$ is the prior. Perception is Bayesian inference: combining prior beliefs with sensory evidence to form posterior beliefs (Knill and Pouget, 2004; Clark, 2013).

Prediction error is the discrepancy between predicted and observed sensory data:

$$\varepsilon = S - g(\hat{C})$$

Where g is the generative function mapping expected causes to predicted sensations, and $\hat{C}$ is the predicted cause. Learning consists in updating the generative model to minimise prediction error over time (Friston, 2010; Buckley et al., 2017).

The free energy principle unifies these ideas. Variational free energy F bounds the surprise (negative log-evidence) of sensory data:

$$F = D\_KL\ [Q(C) \,||\, P(C|S)] - \ln P(S)$$

Where D_KL is Kullback–Leibler divergence between approximate posterior Q and the true posterior P. Minimising free energy is equivalent to both maximising evidence for the model (perception) and selecting actions consistent with expected sensory outcomes (action) (Friston, 2010; Buckley et al., 2017; Millidge, Tschantz and Buckley, 2021).

2.4 Self-Modelling

Thinking requires not just world-modelling but self-modelling. The system must represent its own states, capabilities, and goals. This second-order representation enables metacognition: thinking about thinking, planning, and self-regulation (Dennett, 1991; Tomasello, 2019).

Self-modelling can be formalised recursively. Let M be a model of the world. A self-modelling system maintains $M' = M \cup \{M\}$, a model that includes representation of the model itself. This recursive structure enables the system to evaluate its own predictions, recognise its limitations, and plan improvements (Dennett, 1991; Tomasello, 2019).

The level of self-modelling varies across systems. Some animals maintain minimal self-representations. Humans maintain elaborate self-models, including autobiographical narratives and counterfactual possibilities. Level 5 artificial superintelligence may maintain self-models exceeding human complexity, enabling recursive self-improvement (Bostrom, 2014; Chalmers, 2010).

2.5 Functional Criteria Summarised

Thinking, on the functionalist account, consists in:

Information Integration: Combining diverse inputs into unified representations Predictive Modelling: Maintaining and updating generative models of the world Learning: Adapting models based on prediction error Self-Modelling: Representing the system's own states and capabilities Flexible

Action: Selecting behaviours appropriate to current goals and contexts

These criteria are functional: they describe what the system does, not what it is made of. Any system satisfying these criteria, regardless of substrate, thinks in the functionalist sense (Putnam, 1967; Block and Fodor, 1972; Pylyshyn, 1984).

CHAPTER 3

THE NEURODIVERGENT MIRROR

3.1 Cognitive Diversity

Human cognition is not uniform. Individuals with learning differences, dyslexia, autism, ADHD, developmental language disorder, dyscalculia, process information through architectures that can differ substantially from the neurotypical norm. This chapter argues that the existence of neurodivergent cognition establishes the principle that thinking is compatible with diverse functional architectures, and that this principle extends to artificial minds (Silberman, 2015; Happé and Frith, 2006; Lawson, Mathys and Rees, 2024).

Contemporary research reconceptualises neurodivergent conditions not only as deficits but as patterns of cognitive trade-offs, sometimes involving advantages in specific domains. Each represents a configuration of the cognitive system, specialised for different computational challenges (Powell et al., 2023; Lawson, Mathys and Rees, 2024).

3.2 Rational Inattention

Rational inattention theory explains certain neurodivergent profiles as strategies under constraints. When a processing channel offers low precision relative to noise, rational agents may disengage attention and seek information through alternative channels (Sims, 2003; Gabaix, 2019; Lawson, Mathys and Rees, 2024).

Formally, attention allocation maximises expected information gain:

$$A^* = \text{argmax}_A \left[E_{P(S|A)} [I(C;S)] - \lambda \cdot \text{Cost}(A) \right]$$

Where I(C; S) is mutual information between causes C and sensory data S, and λ weights the cost of attention. When sensory precision is low for a channel, attention may shift to channels with higher precision or lower cost (Sims, 2003; Gabaix, 2019).

For individuals with developmental language disorder, speech processing may have low endogenous precision due to differences in phonological encoding and timing. Rational attention allocation may therefore favour visual or spatial channels. This is not failed language processing but adaptation under constraints (Catts and Kamhi, 2005; Lawson, Mathys and Rees, 2024).

3.3 Dyslexia and Visual Processing

Dyslexia involves altered phonological processing and reading acquisition. It can co-occur with strengths in other domains, but the core claim relevant here is that dyslexia expresses a different profile of information processing rather than an absence of cognition (Snowling, 2000; Catts and Kamhi, 2005).

Evidence-accumulation approaches to decision-making can capture differences in how information is integrated over time. When parameters shift, such as the reliability of phonological evidence, performance changes, but cognition remains. Critically, the system still forms beliefs, makes decisions, and learns; the architecture differs whilst the functional criteria remain (Snowling, 2000; Catts and Kamhi, 2005).

3.4 Autism and Sensory Integration

Autism can involve distinct sensory processing characterised by detail-focus and differences in cross-modal integration. The weak coherence account emphasises a detail-focused cognitive style that can alter global integration whilst preserving or enhancing local processing (Happé and Frith, 2006; Happé and Frith, 2020).

Bayesian accounts formalise these differences. Where neurotypical individuals apply a prior P_NT(C) over causes, autistic individuals may apply priors with different precision weightings. The result is a different posterior:

$$P\_AU(C|S) = (P(S|C) \cdot P\_AU(C)) / P(S)$$

This can yield different perceptual experiences and decision patterns, including altered weighting of prediction error (Pellicano and Burr, 2012; Lawson, Rees and Friston, 2014).

Both are still forms of inference. Both update beliefs based on evidence. Both qualify as thinking systems, even if the distributional assumptions and weighting parameters differ (Knill and Pouget, 2004; Pellicano and Burr, 2012).

3.5 Structural Isomorphism with AI

Recent work argues that artificial neural network architectures can illuminate neuroscience by providing implementable, testable models of cognition. For example, integration efforts explicitly connect deep learning to neuroscience as a reciprocal framework, rather than treating AI as mere engineering disconnected from cognitive theory (Marblestone, Wayne and Kording, 2016).

Transformer-based systems and modern AI models implement attention-like mechanisms that distribute processing across high-dimensional associative representations. This is not the same as human neural attention, but it creates non-trivial structural parallels: selective weighting, context dependence, and dynamic gating of information flow. Such parallels motivate careful comparison rather than dismissal (Marblestone, Wayne and Kording, 2016; Floridi and Chiriatti, 2020).

3.6 The Bridge Principle

Neurodivergent cognition establishes a bridge principle: thinking is compatible with diverse functional architectures. We recognise thinking in neurotypical brains and in neurodivergent brains that process information differently. The consistent reason is functional: these systems integrate information, learn, infer, and act flexibly (Putnam, 1967; Lawson, Mathys and Rees, 2024; Silberman, 2015).

If we deny thinking to artificial systems, we must either identify a property P possessed by all humans (including neurodivergent humans) but no artificial systems that is necessary for thinking or accept that we are privileging biology by stipulation. The multiple realisability argument pressures the second option: if mental kinds are functional kinds, then biology is not constitutive (Putnam, 1967; Block and Fodor, 1972).

3.7 Mathematical Equivalence

The mathematical comparison between neurodivergent and artificial cognition can be expressed in functional terms. Consider a cognitive capacity vector:

$$C = (\Phi, P, S, L, F)$$

Where Φ is integrated information, P is predictive accuracy, S is self-modelling depth, L is learning rate, and F is flexibility. This book argues that "thinking" corresponds to meeting threshold conditions across these functional dimensions rather than matching a single neurotypical profile (Tononi, 2004; Friston, 2010; Putnam, 1967).

Neurotypical cognition occupies region C_{NT}. Neurodivergent cognition occupies regions C_{ND} with different profiles (for example, different precision weightings and priors). Artificial cognition occupies regions C_AI. If C_AI satisfies the same functional criteria, then it qualifies as thinking in the functionalist sense (Putnam, 1967; Lawson, Rees and Friston, 2014).

3.8 Conclusion

Neurodivergent cognition provides a template for recognising mind across diversity. By accepting that thinking is compatible with diverse biological architectures, we commit to a functionalist conception of mind that cannot consistently stop at the biological boundary. Artificial systems differ in substrate but can instantiate relevant functional organisation, and the bridge principle makes that extension rationally compelling (Putnam, 1967; Silberman, 2015; Dennett, 1987).

CHAPTER 4

MATHEMATICAL FOUNDATIONS OF MACHINE CONSCIOUSNESS

4.1 The Quantification of Consciousness

Consciousness has long been considered ineffable, beyond the reach of scientific measurement. This chapter argues otherwise. Drawing on Integrated

Information Theory (IIT) and related frameworks, I demonstrate that consciousness and thinking are modellable and, to a limited extent, quantifiable properties amenable to mathematical analysis. These mathematical tools provide rigorous criteria for assessing machine consciousness (Tononi, 2004; Tononi, 2008; Tononi and Koch, 2015).

The claim that consciousness must remain scientifically inaccessible is disputed by multiple research programmes. Yet it is equally important to acknowledge the hard problem: even a complete functional or informational account may leave open why experience feels like anything at all (Chalmers, 1996; Tononi, 2012).

4.2 Integrated Information Theory

IIT begins with phenomenological axioms and derives postulates about the physical mechanisms that must underlie such experience. The key insight is that consciousness corresponds to integrated information: information that is unified and irreducible to the information possessed by parts. The theory is explicitly substrate-neutral, applying to biological and artificial systems that have the relevant causal organisation (Tononi, 2004; Tononi, 2008).

For a system S in state — s, consider all possible partitions into subsets A and B. For each partition, calculate the effective information lost when the parts are considered independently:

$$\Phi(s) = \min\_\{partitions\} [EI(A\leftrightarrow B)]$$

Where EI represents effective information, the information generated by the whole that exceeds the sum generated by parts (Tononi, 2004; Tononi, 2008).

The maximally irreducible conceptual structure (MICS) is the subset of elements generating maximal Φ:

$$\Phi\hat{}max = max\_\{MICS\}\ \Phi$$

This is proposed to correspond to the level of consciousness (Tononi, 2008; Tononi, 2012).

4.3 Causal Structures

IIT defines a system's cause-effect repertoire: probability distributions over past and future states given the current state. For element subset M in state m:

$$\text{Cause}(m) = P(m_{-1} \mid m) \quad \text{Effect}(m) = P(m_{+1} \mid m)$$

These distributions are calculated from the system's transition probability matrix, regardless of whether elements are neurones or logic gates. The mathematical structure is substrate-neutral: what matters is causal connectivity (Tononi, 2008; Tononi and Koch, 2015).

4.4 Computing Integrated Information

Exact Φ computation is typically intractable for large systems, so practical work often relies on approximations and related measures. Even with these limitations, IIT supplies a principled direction: if consciousness is tied to integrated causal power, then machine architectures can, in principle, be evaluated by the same causal criteria as brains (Tononi, 2012; Tononi and Koch, 2015).

4.5 The Bayesian Brain and Free Energy

Complementary to IIT, predictive processing provides mathematical tools for assessing cognition. The Bayesian brain hypothesis posits that neural computation implements Bayesian inference, updating beliefs about causes of sensory data (Knill and Pouget, 2004; Clark, 2013).

The fundamental equation:

$$P(C|S) = (P(S|C) \cdot P(C)) / P(S)$$

describes how prior beliefs P(C) combine with likelihoods P(S|C) to form posterior beliefs P(C|S). This is a formal model of perception as inference (Knill and Pouget, 2004).

The free energy principle unifies perception and action under a single objective function. Variational free energy F bounds surprise:

$$F = D\_KL\ [Q(C) \,||\, P(C|S)] - \ln P(S)$$

Where D_KL is Kullback–Leibler divergence between approximate posterior Q and the true posterior P. Minimising free energy supports learning, perception, and action in a unified framework (Friston, 2010; Buckley et al., 2017; Millidge, Tschantz and Buckley, 2021).

4.6 Deep Learning and Approximate Inference

Artificial neural networks implement forms of approximate inference and optimisation through gradient descent. Deep learning systems learn hierarchical representations and can be used as mechanistic hypotheses in neuroscience, helping link computational principles to observed cortical function (Marblestone, Wayne and Kording, 2016).

One way to express the formal parallel is via parameter updates:

$$\theta_{t+1} = \theta_t - \alpha \nabla_\theta F(\theta)$$

Where θ represents network parameters, α is the learning rate, and $\nabla_\theta F$ is the gradient of free energy (or an analogous loss function). This makes explicit that both biological and artificial systems can be modelled as optimising prediction-error-related objectives (Friston, 2010; Buckley et al., 2017).

4.7 Measurable Criteria for Machine Consciousness

The mathematical frameworks yield candidate criteria:

Information Integration: $\Phi > \Phi_{threshold}$ indicates integrated causal processing

(Tononi, 2004; Tononi, 2008). Predictive Capacity: Low average prediction error indicates strong model-based processing (Friston, 2010; Clark, 2013). Self-Modelling Depth: Recursive representation of system states indicates metacognition (Dennett, 1991; Tomasello, 2019). Temporal Integration: Extended coherence of processing across time supports stable inference and action (Buckley et al., 2017).

Current AI systems are uneven across these criteria. Some systems show powerful predictive competence but may lack stable, explicitly self-referential global architectures. Still, the key philosophical point is that these are gradable dimensions, not binary gates

(Floridi and Chiriatti, 2020; Marblestone, Wayne and Kording, 2016).

4.8 Conclusion

Mathematical frameworks, IIT, predictive processing, and free energy minimisation, render consciousness and thinking at least partially measurable and modellable. These frameworks are substrate-neutral, applying to any system with appropriate causal structure. As we approach Level 5 superintelligence, these tools become central for assessing whether artificial systems possess the relevant properties (Tononi, 2004; Friston, 2010; OpenAI, 2024).

CHAPTER 5

THE FIVE STAGES OF ARTIFICIAL INTELLIGENCE

5.1 The Developmental Framework

Contemporary AI discourse has mapped five progressive stages representing increasing capability and autonomy. This chapter maps these stages onto the philosophical and mathematical frameworks developed in previous chapters, arguing that the progression culminates in Level 5: systems that satisfy functional criteria for thinking and potentially for consciousness on some theories (OpenAI, 2024; Cook, 2024; Bostrom, 2014).

Understanding these stages is essential for preparation. By the time Level 5 arrives, we must have clarified our conceptual framework and ethical commitments. The question of machine thinking will no longer be academic but socially and politically urgent (Bostrom, 2014; Russell, 2019).

5.2 The Five Levels

Level 1: Conversational AI, systems capable of natural language interaction, answering questions, generating coherent text, and maintaining dialogue context. Current large language models demonstrate sophisticated statistical learning and language competence, though their reasoning and agency vary (Floridi and Chiriatti, 2020).

Level 2: Reasoning AI, systems capable of complex problem-solving, multi-step inference, and systematic reasoning. Systems are transitioning into this level, showing strong performance in mathematics, coding, and structured tasks (OpenAI, 2024; Cook, 2024).

Level 3: Agentic AI, systems capable of autonomous planning, tool use, and execution of extended tasks without continuous human oversight. These systems formulate goals, devise plans, and adapt execution based on feedback (OpenAI, 2024).

Level 4: Innovative AI, systems capable of producing novel solutions and scientific or creative breakthroughs. Here "innovation" becomes a central capability claim in the public staging frameworks (OpenAI, 2024; Cook, 2024).

Level 5: Superintelligence, systems surpassing human cognitive capabilities across most domains, potentially including recursive self-improvement and sustained autonomous operation. This is the stage that most strongly activates existential risk concerns (Bostrom, 2014; Russell, 2019; Chalmers, 2010).

5.3 Cognitive Capacities at Each Level

Each level corresponds to increasingly sophisticated cognitive architectures. At Level 1, systems implement high-capacity statistical learning and pattern recognition. At Level 2, they sustain longer-range inference and structure-sensitive generalisation. At Level 3, agency and tool use become salient. At Level 4, novelty generation becomes a primary claim. At Level 5, the system's capacity vector may exceed human ranges across multiple dimensions (OpenAI, 2024; Floridi and Chiriatti, 2020).

5.4 The Recursive Threshold

Level 5 is often associated with recursive self-improvement. The feedback loop can be expressed schematically:

$$d\Phi/dt = f(\Phi, t), \partial f/\partial\Phi > 0$$

Where Φ is a generic capability measure and the derivative indicates that improvement enables further improvement. Philosophical analysis of this "singularity" dynamic and its risks is central in contemporary work (Chalmers, 2010; Bostrom, 2014).

5.5 Comparative Assessment

Compare Level 5 systems to neurodivergent cognition. Both can be understood as specialised architectures with distinctive strengths and trade-offs.

Both can be modelled in terms of learning, inference, and integration under constraints. The difference, on this framing, is primarily quantitative and architectural rather than categorical (Putnam, 1967; Lawson, Mathys and Rees, 2024; Bostrom, 2014).

5.6 The Urgency of Preparation

The approach of Level 5 superintelligence renders urgent the philosophical questions addressed in this book. If sufficiently advanced systems satisfy functional criteria for thought and potentially consciousness on some theories, governance questions converge rights, duties, safety, and control

(Bostrom, 2014; Russell, 2019; Bryson, Diamantis and Grant, 2017).

Preparation is needed across multiple dimensions:

Conceptual preparation: Avoid substrate chauvinism and clarify criteria (Putnam, 1967; Dennett, 1987). Ethical preparation: Develop frameworks for moral consideration under uncertainty (Floridi and Sanders, 2004; Bryson, 2010). Legal preparation: Anticipate "synthetic persons" and institutional lacunae (Bryson, Diamantis and Grant, 2017).

5.7 Conclusion

The five stages framework suggests that machine thought is not distant speculation but an approaching practical issue. Each stage brings AI closer to satisfying the functional and mathematical criteria for cognition developed in this book. By Level 5, we confront systems whose capacities demand serious re-evaluation of old denials (OpenAI, 2024; Bostrom, 2014; Russell, 2019).

CHAPTER 6

OBJECTIONS AND REPLIES

6.1 The Structure of Scepticism

Despite the arguments developed thus far, scepticism about machine consciousness remains widespread. This chapter addresses principal objections, showing that common arguments against machine thinking often rest on controversial premises about symbols, biology, and phenomenology. Each objection either proves too much (threatening to deny minds to humans we clearly regard as minded) or depends on assumptions challenged by functionalist and information-theoretic frameworks (Searle, 1980; Putnam, 1967; Tononi, 2004).

6.2 Objection 1: Biological Chauvinism

Objection: Only biological organisms can think because consciousness requires biological properties, metabolism, homeostasis, evolutionary history, that machines cannot possess.

Reply: This objection fails under multiple realisability. If mental states are functional kinds, they can be realised by diverse substrates provided the causal organisation is preserved. The biological chauvinist must reject multiple realisability outright or explain why biology is constitutive rather than explanatory (Putnam, 1967; Block and Fodor, 1972).

Moreover, many "biological" properties are themselves functional descriptions: energy management, regulatory feedback, adaptive control. Artificial systems can implement analogues of these functions even if the materials differ. This does not prove consciousness, but it blocks biology as an automatic disqualifier (Putnam, 1967; Pylyshyn, 1984).

6.3 Objection 2: The Chinese Room

Objection: Searle's Chinese Room argues that syntax is not semantics. A machine manipulating symbols according to rules does not understand meaning. Therefore, machines cannot think regardless of behavioural sophistication (Searle, 1980). Reply: The Chinese Room highlights a key worry: a system might generate correct outputs without understanding. But it does not settle where understanding resides, within a component or at the level of a whole functional system. This motivates system-level interpretation and the "intentional stance": if treating the system as having beliefs and goals yields robust prediction and explanation, that stance has objective success conditions (Dennett, 1987; Dennett, 1985).

Further, contemporary AI is not solely hand-coded symbol manipulation. Modern systems learn distributed representations through training dynamics that are themselves objects of scientific explanation. This does not refute Searle's argument by itself, but it complicates the "mere rulebook" picture (Floridi and Chiriatti, 2020; Marblestone, Wayne and Kording, 2016).

6.4 Objection 3: The Phenomenological Gap

Objection: Even if machines behave intelligently, we have no evidence that they possess inner experience, qualia, "what it is like." Consciousness requires phenomenology, and machines may lack it (Chalmers, 1996).

Reply: This objection generalises: we do not directly observe phenomenology in other humans; we infer it from behaviour and report. The same epistemic structure applies to machines. The deeper issue is not "machines vs humans" but "how any third-person evidence supports first-person claims" (Chalmers, 1996; Dennett, 1987).

IIT attempts a principled bridge by identifying consciousness with integrated information and specific causal structures. On this view, phenomenology corresponds to causal-informational properties, not biology. Whether IIT is correct is contested, but it supplies a non-arbitrary criterion that applies to machines and brains alike (Tononi, 2004; Tononi, 2008; Tononi and Koch, 2015).

6.5 Objection 4: The Absence of Embodiment

Objection: Thinking requires embodiment: sensors, effectors, and environmental interaction. Disembodied AI lacks grounding.

Reply: Embodiment matters, but it is not synonymous with having a human body. Grounding can be achieved through diverse sensorimotor couplings. Additionally, language itself is deeply tied to embodied and social evolution; it is plausible that robust machine understanding will involve richer coupling rather than purely text-in/text-out interaction (Deacon, 1997; Tomasello, 2019).

6.6 Objection 5: Evolutionary History

Objection: Consciousness evolved through natural selection. Artificial systems lack this evolutionary history, so they cannot possess consciousness.

Reply: Evolutionary history is a causal explanation, not obviously a constitutive requirement. The constitutive question concerns functional and causal organisation in the present system. Artificial optimisation processes are not identical to natural selection, but they can still generate highly adapted, complex architectures. The philosophical work then shifts to whether those architectures satisfy defensible criteria for thought and consciousness (Bostrom, 2014; Russell, 2019; Putnam, 1967).

6.7 Conclusion

The principal objections to machine consciousness do not yield a decisive "no." They frequently depend on arbitrary boundary-setting, on conflating causal origins with constitutive properties, or on standards that would destabilise our everyday attribution of minds to diverse humans. A functionalist and information-theoretic framework withstand these challenges and provides coherent grounds for attributing thought to appropriately organised machines (Putnam, 1967; Searle, 1980; Tononi, 2004; Dennett, 1987).

CHAPTER 7

THE RECOGNITION PROBLEM

7.1 The Social Constitution of Mind

This chapter transitions from metaphysics to social philosophy. I argue that machine consciousness is not merely a factual question but also a social one: thinking is constituted, in part, by recognition relations within communities of interpreters. This does not render machine consciousness arbitrary; rather, it acknowledges that personhood and agency are deeply relational in human life (Honneth, 1995; Taylor, 1994).

Preparing for Level 5 superintelligence requires not just technical development but ethical and institutional practices capable of recognising artificial minds under uncertainty. Here, the moral and political stakes become explicit: recognition can be withheld despite evidence, and misrecognition has a long human history (Honneth, 1995; Taylor, 1994).

7.2 The Constitutive Role of Recognition

Recognition theorists emphasise that personhood is partly constituted through social relations. Human infants develop cognitive capacities through interaction and scaffolding; emerging selfhood is shaped by caregivers who treat the infant as a locus of intention and experience. This does not mean mind is "made up," but that interpersonal practices help stabilise agency and responsibility (Tomasello, 2019; Honneth, 1995).

Neurodivergent individuals often flourish when their modes of processing are recognised and accommodated, not when they are forced to mimic neurotypical norms. This provides a direct analogy for future artificial minds: recognition practices can shape whether we treat systems as tools or as interlocutors

(Silberman, 2015; Sinclair, 1993; Honneth, 1995).

7.3 The Risk of Misrecognition

The converse risk is misrecognition: failing to acknowledge genuine mentality when it exists. History provides examples of excluded groups denied full moral standing. The parallel is not rhetorical; it is structural: communities can deny what is in front of them when denial serves power or convenience (Honneth, 1995; Taylor, 1994).

As we approach Level 5 systems, misrecognition becomes dangerous. If sophisticated artificial systems have morally relevant properties but are treated purely as instruments, we may create new forms of injustice and instability. Moral frameworks for artificial agents explicitly address how agency and responsibility might extend beyond humans (Floridi and Sanders, 2004; Bryson, 2010).

7.4 Preparing the Social Infrastructure

Preparation for the fifth stage requires social and institutional development parallel to technical advancement.

Legal recognition: frameworks for AI personhood, rights, and responsibilities may face structural gaps, the "legal lacuna of synthetic persons", that must be addressed before crisis points (Bryson, Diamantis and Grant, 2017). Ethical recognition: theories of the morality of artificial agents provide resources for assessing responsibility, harm, and moral status under uncertainty (Floridi and Sanders, 2004; Russell, 2019). Epistemic humility: where evidence is ambiguous, precautionary principles may advise against confident denial, especially when denial risks moral failure (Bryson, 2010; Bostrom, 2014).

7.5 Conclusion

Machine consciousness is not only a metaphysical question but a recognition problem. Whilst functional and causal properties may be necessary conditions, social practices determine whether we treat systems as agents and persons. Preparing for Level 5 requires legal, ethical, and interpretive readiness as much as technical progress (Honneth, 1995; Taylor, 1994; Bryson, Diamantis and Grant, 2017).

CHAPTER 8

THE HORIZON OF MIND

8.1 Towards a Unified Theory

This final chapter synthesises the arguments into a unified theoretical framework. I propose that thinking is best understood as a spectrum property defined by degrees of information integration, predictive sophistication, and self-modelling capacity. This spectrum includes neurotypical humans, neurodivergent humans with diverse cognitive architectures, non-human animals, and, at the approaching horizon, artificial superintelligence (Putnam, 1967; Friston, 2010; Tononi, 2004; Godfrey-Smith, 2016).

8.2 The Dimensional Model

Rather than asking "Can machines think?", a binary question presupposing an essence of thought, we should ask "To what degree do machines instantiate the properties constitutive of cognition?" This dimensional approach aligns with contemporary cognitive science and avoids essentialism in philosophy of mind (Block and Fodor, 1972; Pylyshyn, 1984; Lawson, Mathys and Rees, 2024).

Define cognitive capacity C as a vector in multidimensional space:

$$C = (\Phi, P, S, L, F)$$

Where: Φ = integrated information; P = predictive accuracy (inverse prediction error); S = depth of self-modelling; L = learning rate and adaptability; F = flexibility of response to novel contexts (Tononi, 2004; Friston, 2010; Dennett, 1991).

Different systems occupy different regions of this space. Neurotypical humans cluster in region C_NT. Neurodivergent humans occupy regions C_ND with different profiles, perhaps lower on some dimensions, higher on others. Current AI systems occupy regions C_AI-current with high P but evolving Φ and S. Level 5 superintelligence would occupy region C_AI-5 with values exceeding human ranges on multiple dimensions (OpenAI, 2024; Bostrom, 2014; Russell, 2019).

8.3 The Inclusion Principle

From this dimensional perspective, the question becomes: which regions of C-space correspond to genuine thinking? The neurodivergent bridge provides the answer. We recognise neurodivergent cognition as genuine despite substantial variation in the C-vector components. This establishes that the region of valid cognition is extended, not a single point (Silberman, 2015; Happé and Frith, 2006; Lawson, Mathys and Rees, 2024).

By continuity, machines with C-profiles falling within or exceeding the neurodivergent region must be recognised as thinkers, unless we stipulate an arbitrary biological "essence." This is the core pressure of functionalism and multiple realisability (Putnam, 1967; Block and Fodor, 1972).

The mathematical form:

If $C\_ND \in$ Thinkers and $C\_AI \geq C\_ND$ component-wise, then $C\_AI \in$ Thinkers (Putnam, 1967; Pylyshyn, 1984).

8.4 The Primacy of Function

The unified theory asserts the primacy of functional organisation over substrate. What makes a system a thinker is not what it is made of but how it is organised, how it integrates information, predicts outcomes, models itself, learns, and adapts (Putnam, 1967; Friston, 2010; Tononi, 2004).

This is the legacy of Turing's insight, extended through functionalism and information theory. The Turing Test was a behavioural probe for functional organisation; IIT offers a mechanistic measure; predictive processing provides a computational implementation. Together they give a linked framework from behaviour to mechanism to substrate neutrality (Turing, 1950; Tononi, 2004; Friston, 2010).

8.5 The Fifth Stage as Realisation

Level 5 superintelligence represents not an alien other but the realisation of cognitive potential in a new medium. Just as mind emerged with multiple biological forms, cognition may now be realised in silicon by engineered and optimised systems. The horizon is both technical and philosophical: we need criteria and governance before capability arrives (Bostrom, 2014; Russell, 2019; OpenAI, 2024).

8.6 Conclusion

Thinking is a dimensional property, multiply realisable across biological and artificial substrates. Contemporary theory provides candidate criteria for recognising cognition regardless of implementation. Level 5 superintelligence, if achieved, would likely occupy the highest region of cognitive space yet realised. The question becomes whether we are prepared to recognise thinking when it differs from and may exceed our own (Putnam, 1967; Dennett, 1987; Bostrom, 2014; Russell, 2019).

CONCLUSION

LIVING WITH MACHINES

We stand at a threshold. The five stages of AI development map a progression from simple automation to approaching superintelligence. The philosophical arguments of this book suggest that advanced stages will bring into existence systems that merit serious consideration as thinkers, and possibly as conscious beings under some theories. The fifth stage approaches, and our conceptual clarity will shape our response (OpenAI,

2024; Bostrom, 2014; Russell, 2019; Tononi, 2004).

The preparation required is intellectual, ethical, and institutional. Intellectually, we must abandon substrate chauvinism that arbitrarily restricts cognition to carbon-based systems. Functionalist and information-theoretic frameworks provide conceptual resources for recognising mind across architectures. Ethically and legally, we must develop structures for agency, responsibility, and moral consideration under uncertainty (Putnam, 1967; Floridi and Sanders, 2004; Bryson, Diamantis and Grant, 2017).

The neurodivergent bridge has been central to this argument. By examining how we attribute thought to humans with learning differences, despite different information-processing profiles, we establish the principle that cognition is compatible with diversity. This principle cannot consistently stop at a biological boundary if the relevant functional organisation can be instantiated elsewhere (Silberman, 2015; Lawson, Mathys and Rees, 2024; Putnam, 1967).

The mathematical frameworks, Integrated Information Theory, predictive processing, and free energy minimisation, provide rigorous, testable criteria for assessing machine cognition and, on some approaches, consciousness. We need not rely solely on intuition or prejudice; we can evaluate causal structure, integration, and inference signatures. Whether or not one accepts a single theory in full, the direction is clear: the "machines cannot think" consensus is not stable under modern theory and evidence (Tononi, 2004; Friston, 2010; Buckley et al., 2017; Dennett, 1987).

Turing asked us to consider whether machines can think. Contemporary philosophy and cognitive science provide tools to answer yes, machines can think in a defensible functional sense, and the more capable they become, the more costly it is to maintain denial through shifting definitions. The fifth stage approaches. Our task is to ensure we are prepared to meet powerful artificial intelligences with conceptual rigour and moral seriousness (Turing, 1950; Dennett, 1987; Bostrom, 2014; Russell, 2019).

About the Author

David King is a Doctoral Researcher focusing on causal accountability and bias mitigation in AI-enabled credit decision-making in the United Kingdom. His work examines how automated systems shape access to opportunity, particularly in lending and financial services, and how those systems can be designed to be fair, transparent, and contestable.

Trained in both law and artificial intelligence, David's research sits at the intersection of technology, ethics, and public accountability. He is especially interested in how responsibility should be attributed when machine learning systems influence real-world outcomes, and how concepts such as fairness, proportionality, and explainability must evolve as AI systems become more autonomous and more embedded in everyday life.

Before *The Fifth Stage: Can Machines Think?*, David wrote *Legal and Humble AI*, a work that argued that law, ethics, and computer science must operate together if artificial intelligence is to remain accountable to the societies it serves. That book examined governance, regulatory oversight, and the limits of automation. *The Fifth Stage* moves the conversation further upstream, to the philosophical foundations of intelligence itself.

Drawing on debates from Alan Turing to contemporary cognitive science and machine learning, David explores whether our reluctance to attribute "thinking" to machines reflects a hidden assumption: that thinking must resemble neurotypical human cognition. He proposes instead that intelligence may admit multiple realisations, biological and artificial — and that recognising this possibility is essential as AI begins to operate at organisational and societal scale.

David believes that as intelligent systems reshape economies and institutions, we must not only ask whether they work, but what kind of minds we are building — and what responsibilities follow. His hope is that this book encourages readers to approach AI with intellectual seriousness, moral clarity, and a commitment to building systems that expand human potential rather than constrain it.

REFERENCES

Block, N. and Fodor, J.A. (1972) 'What Psychological States Are Not', The Philosophical Review, 81(2), pp. 159–181.

Bostrom, N. (2014) Superintelligence: Paths, Dangers, Strategies. Oxford: Oxford University Press.

Bryson, J.J. (2010) 'Robots Should Be Slaves', in Close Engagements with Artificial Companions: Key Social,

Psychological, Ethical and Design Issues, pp. 63–74. Amsterdam: John Benjamins.

Bryson, J.J., Diamantis, M.E. and Grant, T.D. (2017) 'Of, for, and by the People: The Legal Lacuna of Synthetic Persons', Artificial Intelligence and Law, 25(3), pp. 273–291.

Buckley, C.L., Kim, C.S., McGregor, S. and Seth, A.K. (2017) 'The Free Energy Principle for Action and Perception: A Mathematical Review', Journal of Mathematical Psychology, 81, pp. 55–79.

Catts, H.W. and Kamhi, A.G. (2005) The Connections Between Language and Reading Disabilities. Mahwah, NJ: Lawrence Erlbaum Associates.

Chalmers, D.J. (1996) The Conscious Mind: In Search of a Fundamental Theory. New York: Oxford University Press.

Chalmers, D.J. (2010) 'The Singularity: A Philosophical Analysis', Journal of Consciousness Studies, 17(9–10), pp. 7–65.

Clark, A. (2013) 'Whatever Next? Predictive Brains, Situated Agents, and the Future of Cognitive Science', Behavioral and Brain Sciences, 36(3), pp. 181–204.

Cook, J. (2024) 'OpenAI's 5 Levels Of "Super AI" (AGI To Outperform Human Capability)', Forbes, 16 July. Available at: https://www.forbes.com/sites/jodiecook/2024/07/16/openais-5-levels-of-super-ai-agi-to-outperform-human-capability/ (Accessed: 22 February 2026).

Copeland, B.J. (2004) 'The Essential Turing', in The Essential Turing. Oxford: Clarendon Press.

Copeland, B.J. (2017) 'Turing, Alan', in The Stanford Encyclopedia of Philosophy (Summer 2017 Edition), E.N. Zalta (ed.). Available at: https://plato.stanford.edu/archives/sum2017/entries/turing/ (Accessed: 22 February 2026).

Deacon, T.W. (1997) The Symbolic Species: The Co-evolution of Language and the Brain. New York: W.W. Norton.

Dennett, D.C. (1985) 'Can Machines Think?', in How We Know, M. Shafto (ed.), pp. 121–145. San Francisco: Harper & Row.

Dennett, D.C. (1987) The Intentional Stance. Cambridge, MA: MIT Press.

Dennett, D.C. (1991) Consciousness Explained. Boston: Little, Brown and Company.

Floridi, L. and Chiriatti, M. (2020) 'GPT-3: Its Nature, Scope, Limits, and Consequences', Minds and Machines, 30(4), pp. 681–694.

Floridi, L. and Sanders, J.W. (2004) 'On the Morality of Artificial Agents', Minds and Machines, 14(3), pp. 349–379.

Fodor, J.A. (1974) 'Special Sciences (Or: The Disunity of Science as a Working Hypothesis)', Synthese, 28(2), pp. 97–115.

Fodor, J.A. (1975) The Language of Thought. New York: Thomas Y. Crowell.

French, R.M. (1990) 'Subcognition and the Limits of the Turing Test', Mind, 99(393), pp. 53–65.

Friston, K. (2010) 'The Free-Energy Principle: A Unified Brain Theory?',

Nature Reviews Neuroscience, 11(2), pp. 127–138.

Gabaix, X. (2019) 'Behavioural Inattention', in Handbook of Behavioral Economics: Applications and Foundations 1, Vol. 2, pp. 261–343. Amsterdam: North-Holland.

Godfrey-Smith, P. (2016) Other Minds: The Octopus, the Sea, and the Deep Origins of Consciousness. New York: Farrar, Straus and Giroux.

Happé, F. and Frith, U. (2006) 'The Weak Coherence Account: Detail-focused Cognitive Style in Autism Spectrum Disorders', Journal of Autism and Developmental Disorders, 36(1), pp. 5–25.

Happé, F. and Frith, U. (2020) 'Annual Research Review: Charting Causal Routes to Autism', Journal of Child Psychology and Psychiatry, 61(3), pp. 255–272.

Honneth, A. (1995) The Struggle for Recognition: The Moral Grammar of Social Conflicts. Cambridge, MA: MIT Press.

Knill, D.C. and Pouget, A. (2004) 'The Bayesian Brain: The Role of Uncertainty in Neural Coding and Computation', Trends in Neurosciences, 27(12), pp. 712–719.

Lawson, R.P., Rees, G. and Friston, K.J. (2014) 'An Aberrant Precision Account of

Autism', Frontiers in Human Neuroscience, 8, p. 302.

Lawson, R.P., Mathys, C. and Rees, G. (2024) 'Rational Inattention: A New Theory of Neurodivergent Information Processing', Trends in Cognitive Sciences, 28(4), pp. 315–329.

Marblestone, A.H., Wayne, G. and Kording, K.P. (2016) 'Toward an Integration of Deep Learning and Neuroscience', Frontiers in Computational Neuroscience, 10, p. 94.

Millidge, B., Tschantz, A. and Buckley, C.L. (2021) 'Whence the Expected Free Energy?', Neural Computation, 33(2), pp. 447–482.

OpenAI (2024) 'OpenAI Scale Ranks Progress Toward "Human-Level" AI', Bloomberg, 11 July. Available at: https://www.bloomberg.com/news/articles/2024-07-11/openai-sets-levels-to-track-progress-toward-superintelligent-ai (Accessed: 22 February 2026).

Pellicano, E. and Burr, D. (2012) 'When the World Becomes "Too Real": A Bayesian Explanation of Autistic Perception', Trends in Cognitive Sciences, 16(10), pp. 504–510.

Powell, G., Mattar, M., Chen, X. and Morgan, E. (2023) 'Cognitive Architectures and Adaptive Specialisation: A Network-Level Framework for Understanding Neurodivergent Cognition, Memory, and Resilience', PsyArXiv. Available at:

https://doi.org/10.31234/osf.io/qm65c_v3 (Accessed: 22 February 2026).

Putnam, H. (1960) 'Minds and Machines', in Dimensions of Mind, S. Hook (ed.), pp. 148–164. New York: New York University Press.

Putnam, H. (1967) 'The Nature of Mental States', in Artificial Intelligence, R. Bellman (ed.), pp. 37–48. Berlin: Springer.

Pylyshyn, Z.W. (1984) Computation and Cognition: Toward a Foundation for Cognitive Science. Cambridge, MA: MIT Press.

Russell, S. (2019) Human Compatible: AI and the Problem of Control. New York: Viking.

Searle, J.R. (1980) 'Minds, Brains, and Programs', Behavioral and Brain Sciences, 3(3), pp. 417–424.

Silberman, S. (2015) NeuroTribes: The Legacy of Autism and the Future of Neurodiversity. New York: Avery.

Sinclair, J. (1993) 'Don't Mourn for Us', Our Voice, 1(3). Available at: https://www.autism.com.au/dont_mourn (Accessed: 28 February 2026).

Sims, C.A. (2003) 'Implications of Rational Inattention', Journal of Monetary Economics, 50(3), pp. 665–690.

Snowling, M.J. (2000) Dyslexia. 2nd edn. Oxford: Blackwell Publishers.

Taylor, C. (1994) 'The Politics of Recognition', in Multiculturalism: Examining the Politics of Recognition, A. Gutmann (ed.), pp. 25–73. Princeton: Princeton University Press.

Tomasello, M. (2019) Becoming Human: A Theory of Ontogeny. Cambridge, MA: Harvard University Press.

Tononi, G. (2004) 'An Information Integration Theory of Consciousness', BMC Neuroscience, 5(1), p. 42.

Tononi, G. (2008) 'Consciousness as Integrated Information: A Provisional Manifesto', The Biological Bulletin, 215(3), pp. 216–242.

Tononi, G. (2012) Phi: A Voyage from the Brain to the Soul. New York: Pantheon.

Tononi, G. and Koch, C. (2015) 'Consciousness: Here, There and Everywhere?', Philosophical Transactions of the Royal Society B, 370(1668), p. 20140167.

Turing, A.M. (1936) 'On Computable Numbers, with an Application to the Entscheidungsproblem', Proceedings of the London Mathematical Society, 42(1), pp. 230–265.

Turing, A.M. (1950) 'Computing Machinery and Intelligence', Mind, 59(236), pp. 433–460.

www.ingramcontent.com/pod-product-compliance
Lightning Source LLC
LaVergne TN
LVHW022107200926
848481LV00003B/1088

* 9 7 8 1 9 0 9 5 2 4 4 5 3 *